Magical Rescue Vets

Suki the Sea Dragon

Melody Lockhart

Titles in this series

1. Oona the Unicorn
2. Jade the Gem Dragon
3. Blaze the Phoenix
4. Holly the Flying Horse
5. Snowball the Baby Yeti
6. Suki the Sea Dragon

This edition published in 2023 by Arcturus Publishing Limited
26/27 Bickels Yard, 151–153 Bermondsey Street,
London SE1 3HA

Author: Melody Lockhart
Story editor: Xanna Eve Chown
Illustrator: Morgan Huff
Designer: Jeni Child
Managing editor: Joe Harris

CH010411NT
Supplier 10, Date 0223, PI 00004096

Printed in the UK

Contents

Starfall Forest Map

WEATHER-OR-NOT CAVES

OH-NO VOLCANOES

COZY CAMPSITE

FAIRGROUND FIELDS

ELFINGTON CASTLE

SOFT HENGE

COTTON-TOP MOUNTAINS

KELP TOWN

LOOKING-GLASS LAKE

CALICO COMFREYS

RAINBOW RIVER

MAZE WOOD

GNOME TOWN

TILTING TOWER

WILLOW COTTAGE

RAINBOW COASTER HILLS

MOONFLOWER MEADOWS

SPRINGHAVEN

TOPSY-TURVY TREES

Chapter 1
Singing Starfish

Kat pressed an ear to the side of the fish tank. "I can't hear anything," she said. "Are you sure they're *singing* starfish?"

"Of course," replied Doctor Hart. "Maybe if I start, they'll join in ... la-la-la-laaa!"

The star-shaped creatures watched the vet as she twirled around. Their tiny mouths formed "o" shapes, but no sound came out.

"Come on, girls! Don't just stand there, join in! La-la-laaa!"

Kat grinned at her best friend, Rosie. "Just a normal Thursday afternoon at Calico Comfrey's!" she laughed.

Kat had lived in the quiet town of Springhaven, on the edge of Starfall Forest, her whole life. But she had only learned the forest's amazing secret when her friend Rosie came to live there too. Starfall was a safe haven for an astonishing number of magical creatures—and Calico Comfrey's Veterinary Surgery helped care for them all. Kat and Rosie loved spending time with the vets. You never knew what sort of animals you'd meet!

The surgery was run by Doctor Hart, a kind old witch with curly hair and large square glasses—and an enthusiasm for singalongs! "Dear me, I think they've lost their voices," she said.

Rosie took a notepad out of her bag and turned to the fishergnome who had brought the starfish in. "Tell us everything that happened," she said.

"It wasn't my fault," gulped the gnome, stroking his beard anxiously. He explained that he had been out fishing on Looking-Glass Lake when he spotted the starfish on the shore. When he tried to help them back into the water, they jumped right out again! "Something in the lake must have scared them," he said. "I couldn't leave them on the sand to dry out, so I put them in my bucket and brought them here."

"You did the right thing," said Doctor Hart. "I can make a Sing-Song Spell that will get them singing again in no time." She opened a cupboard and took out a large jar of purple petals. A sweet, flowery smell filled the room as she spooned some into a flask and added a few drops of water.

"You need three things to make a spell work," said Doctor Hart. "The right ingredients ... the magic words ... and just a little pinch of *je ne sais quoi!*"

"What's that?" asked Kat, puzzled.

"It's French," said Doctor Hart, "for 'I have *absolutely* no idea.' There's just something special inside you when you're a witch! Now, if you give the potion a stir, I'll try to remember what to say. How does it begin? It's either *Sing loud* or *Sing proud* ..."

Kat took a long-handled spoon and

started to stir, making the potion froth up in an alarming way. She jumped backward as the mixture exploded over the top of the flask, hissing and spitting onto the table.

Doctor Hart fetched a cloth to mop up the mess. "Don't worry," she said thoughtfully. "There are lots of reasons a spell can go wrong. Sometimes, there's just too much magic in the air. Let's try this again tomorrow, shall we?"

There was a knock on the door, and Doctor Clarice entered the room. She was the youngest vet at Calico Comfrey's, with long, red hair and round glasses.

"Has anyone seen the socktopus?" she asked, "It's missing again."

"I bet it's in the laundry," said Doctor Hart. "It's always searching for socks to wear. Why don't I look for it while you give the girls a lift home?"

"Great idea!" said Doctor Clarice. Her eyes lit up like they always did when she had been tinkering with one of her amazing machines. "I can show Kat and Rosie my new, extra-bubbly fuel for the flying carpet. It should make the journey twice as fast."

Kat glanced at the clock and groaned. "I can't believe it's time to go home already. There's a spelling bee at school tomorrow

and so many words to learn."

"Bee?" squeaked the fishergnome. "I don't like bees! Nasty, buzzy things."

"Bees are very helpful creatures," laughed Doctor Hart. "But I think Kat is talking about a spelling competition."

Soon the girls were swooping through the air with Doctor Clarice.

"This is great!" yelled Rosie as the forest below flew past in a blur. Kat didn't reply. She was too busy thinking about school.

The carpet landed beside the wrought-iron gate that separated the forest from Rosie's back yard. A clever enchantment meant that only people who were true friends to animals could see it. The gate had been put there by Doctor Hart's grandfather—Calico Comfrey—when he lived in Willow Cottage many years ago. He was the powerful wizard who had first brought all the magical animals to live in Starfall Forest.

"Do you want to stay for dinner?" Rosie asked. "It won't take us long to learn the spellings."

"It'll probably take *me* ages," said Kat gloomily. "I'd better go home."

Kat walked slowly back to her house and found her dad playing basketball with Jordan and Jayden, her twin brothers.

"Hey," Dad called. "Think fast!" He stopped

bouncing the ball and threw it to Kat. She caught it easily and started dribbling it along the driveway.

"Good job, superstar!" cheered Dad.

Kat giggled. Dad always knew how to make her smile. If only there was more basketball at school—and less spelling. She approached the net and prepared to shoot. *Whoosh!* The ball flew straight into the net, and the twins cheered.

Bertie the cat followed Kat into the house and up the stairs to her bedroom. She picked him up and nuzzled her face into his soft fur. Kat's family had lots of pets—one iguana, two cats, four hamsters, and even six chickens in the backyard—but Kat loved them all. With her parents, the twins, and baby Brianna too, things could sometimes get a little crowded, but that was how she liked it.

Bertie curled up at her feet as she opened her spelling book. The letters on the page seemed to swim in front of her eyes. She put the book down. "Do you think spelling bees actually exist, Bertie?" she asked. She imagined a hive full of large, buzzing bees with fuzzy black and yellow letters instead of stripes. "If they did, they'd definitely live in Starfall Forest."

There was a knock on the door, and her

mother came in. "You're home early, Kat," she said. "Is everything okay?"

"I'm no good at spelling," Kat sighed. "I always get the letters mixed up."

"You're probably tired," Mama said. "We had your eyes tested last week and you don't need glasses. Shall I read out the words?"

Kat shook her head. "It's okay," she said. "I'll keep trying."

The next day, Rosie was late for school. She apologized to Miss Lavender, then sat down at her desk. "I've had such a strange morning," she whispered to Kat. "Dad couldn't find any of his socks, and Mama kept saying she could smell seaweed!"

"No talking please," said Miss Lavender. "This is class time, not chat time." She told the children they were going to be making a display for the classroom wall. "Write a paragraph about something you enjoy doing during the weekend, then draw a picture," she said. "Here's mine." She

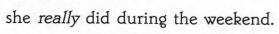

held up a picture she had drawn of herself skydiving.

Kat knew she couldn't draw what she *really* did during the weekend. It was important to keep her visits to the forest a secret to protect the magical creatures that lived there. None of her classmates had ever set foot in Starfall, thanks to the enchanted forget-me-do flowers that grew all around it.

"What are you writing about?" she asked Rosie.

"Playing the piano," Rosie grinned. "What about you?"

"Going to the swimming pool," Kat said. She started drawing wobbly blue lines for the water, then added a big, red water slide.

"Beautiful handwriting, Rosie," said Miss Lavender, who was walking past.

Kat saw that her friend had finished the writing and the picture. How had Rosie managed to do it all so quickly? And why was her handwriting always so neat? Kat's usually looked like a tangled-up ball of string! She picked up her pen and tapped it on the paper. *Splodge!* A little splash of blue ink leaked out.

"I need four students to collect these lovely pictures and stick them on the display board," said Miss Lavender. "Let's see. Dexter, Megan, Lacey, and ... Rosie. Thank you."

Rosie gave Kat a little nudge on her way to collect the sticky tape. "Hurry up," she said. "You haven't written anything yet."

"I know," said Kat pulling a face.

"Sorry," said Rosie. "I'll collect yours last to

give you a bit more time." She looked at Kat's picture. There were lots of children having fun in the water, splashing and diving. "It's very good," she said.

Rosie and the rest of her team started arranging everyone's work on the board. Dexter wanted to put his picture right in the middle—but Lacey thought hers should go there instead! Rosie looked over at Kat and rolled her eyes at how silly they were being.

Then, it was time for the spelling bee.

"Everyone stand up," said Miss Lavender. "If you spell a word wrong, you must sit down. The last one standing is today's champion."

Kat tried to concentrate on what Miss Lavender was saying, but she could hear a faint buzzing noise coming from somewhere in the room. Perhaps spelling bees are real creatures after all, she thought in astonishment. She looked around the classroom. Nobody else seemed to have noticed the buzzing.

Buzzzzzzz. The noise was coming from under her desk near her feet. She glanced down and suddenly realized what it was. She had her crystalzoometer in her backpack! The vets' magical pendant was buzzing to tell her there was an animal in trouble nearby.

"Kat," said Miss Lavender. "Your word is: RHYME."

Kat felt her face turn red as everyone in the room looked at her. "Rhyme," she said slowly. She shut her eyes and tried to picture the letters, but the buzzing noise kept making her think about fuzzy little bees instead. "R ... H ... I ... M ... E. Rhyme."

She heard Lacey Goldstone giggle.

"I'm sorry, Kat," said Miss Lavender. "That's not it."

Kat sat down in her seat. "Excuse me, Miss Lavender," she said. "I feel a little sick. Can I get a glass of water?"

Miss Lavender nodded sympathetically. Kat picked up her bag and ran out of the classroom. In the corridor, she opened the bag and took out the crystalzoometer. Sure enough, it was glowing—but, to her surprise, the needle pointed right back into the room she had just left! What was going on?

By the time Kat returned to the classroom, there were only two students left standing up—Rosie and Dexter. Then Dexter forgot the second C in BROCCOLI ... and Rosie was the winner!

"Well done," Kat whispered, feeling pleased for her friend.

When the bell rang for recess, Miss Lavender asked Kat if she could stay behind for a moment. "Don't worry, you're not in trouble," she said. "I wanted to make sure you were alright."

Kat nodded. "I don't feel sick anymore," she said.

"That's good," said Miss Lavender. "Some people just find spelling a little harder than others, and I think you're one of them. I'd like to arrange a meeting with your parents to see what we can do to help."

Kat's mind was racing as she left the room. Miss Lavender had told her not to worry, but she couldn't help it! What would happen when her parents came in for the meeting? What would Miss Lavender tell them? Would she say that Kat had to move to a different class, or—worse—a different school far away from Rosie and Starfall Forest? It was an awful thought.

She hurried out into the yard and found Rosie deep in conversation with Megan, Lacey, and Dexter. They were talking about the pictures they'd stuck up on the display board.

"I'm learning to play the drums," Megan was saying. "I *used* to play the piano, but it was so boring I gave it up."

"Oh ..." Rosie looked taken aback. "I like it."

"Really?" Lacey raised her eyebrows. "Well, I guess it's okay if you don't have anything *else* to do. I got a pony for my birthday, so I spend all my spare time riding."

"You know what's more fun than piano practice?" joked Dexter. "*Everything!*"

All the children laughed—except Rosie.

It's not fair, Kat thought. Rosie had met a dragon, rescued a unicorn, and even ridden a flying horse ... *She just couldn't tell them.*

Suddenly, Kat noticed something very strange sticking out of her friend's backpack—a little blue tentacle with a stripy sock on the end. An octopus wearing socks? Kat gasped. The missing socktopus! It must have climbed into Rosie's bag yesterday when no one was looking ... No wonder her crystalzoometer had been buzzing!

Kat looked at Megan, Dexter, and Lacey. They were too busy laughing at Dexter's

joke to see the magical creature peeping out at them. She had to do something fast.

"Hi, Rosie," she said loudly. She threw her arms around her friend, using the hug as an excuse to tuck the creature gently back into the bag. "Have you looked in your bag today? I think one of my ... er ... socks is in there."

"It is," said Rosie. "I've seen it." She opened her eyes extra wide and nodded her head to show that she knew *exactly* what Kat was really talking about.

"Is it alright?" Kat asked. "I think it might be in trouble."

"I'm not sure," said Rosie. "Let's take my bag to the cloakroom and check."

Lacey stared after the girls as they hurried away. "That was weird," she said. "Who worries that their socks are in trouble?!"

Rosie sat on a bench in the cloakroom and opened her backpack. Kat peered inside and two tiny eyes blinked back at her from a nest of socks.

"Now we know where all your dad's socks went," gasped Kat. "But ... how long have you known it was in there?"

"I saw it climb into my bag after the spelling bee," said Rosie. "It must have crawled out to look for socks—and come back when it only found ones with feet inside!"

"There's something I'd like to try," Kat said. Carefully, she reached into Rosie's bag and picked up the socktopus. At once, there was a buzzing sound from her pocket.

"Is that your crystalzoometer?" Rosie asked. "I left mine at home."

Kat nodded. "It was buzzing during the spelling bee, too," she said. She put the little creature back into Rosie's bag and the crystalzoometer stopped spinning immediately.

"That's strange," said Rosie. "Is the socktopus in danger or not?"

"Only when it leaves its sock-nest," said Kat.

"Oh my goodness," said Rosie. "It can't live in my bag forever! We'll take it back to the vet's at the end of school."

Chapter 3
Through the Telescope

The surgery was crowded with creatures that usually live in the water. Kat and Rosie stared at a froggle with a rainbow-striped tongue that was croaking noisily at a seapony in the next tank.

"Oh my flags and flippers, we've been so busy," grumbled Doctor Morel. "The crystalzoometers have been buzzing all day— and we *still* haven't found that socktopus. I haven't even had time to water my hat!"

Kat grinned. Doctor Morel was a gnome vet with pointy ears—and an even pointier hat! His hat always seemed to have several mushrooms sprouting out of it, but she'd never heard him talk about watering them before ...

Rosie took the socktopus out of her bag and explained what had happened.

"It's a good job your dad has such nice, comfy socks," said Doctor Morel. "I'll give it a check-up if you two water this trootle for me." He passed Kat a turtle with a tiny tropical island on its shell. "Its palm tree dried up because it was scared to go into the lake."

"Just like the singing starfish!" exclaimed Rosie. "Did they ever get their voices back?"

"Yes," said Doctor Morel. "But I wish they hadn't! They were *completely* out of tune."

"I wonder what's scaring them?" Kat said.

Doctor Morel shrugged. "It's a mystery," he said. "But Doctor Clarice is using the magical spyglasses to look at the lake. She might find a clue ..."

The girls climbed the spiral staircase to the top of the surgery and stepped out onto a large platform. The wooden rail that ran around the edge was covered in telescopes of all shapes and sizes. Doctor Clarice was holding a blue one with a heart-shaped lens.

Kat knew that each telescope did something amazing—from tracking unicorns to making the world look upside-down—all powered by special crystals. She picked up a strange, silvery spyglass.

"That one shows you the forest as it was 1,000 years ago," said Doctor Clarice. "If you're lucky, you might even spot the

Whistling Warlocks who used to live here."

Kat looked through the spyglass and saw three mysterious figures in long,

flowing robes. "I can see them!" she said, excitedly handing Doctor Clarice the telescope. "I think they're casting a spell."

Doctor Clarice took a look. "They could be," she said. "Or they could be whistling a happy tune. You never can tell with the Whistling Warlocks."

Rosie was more interested in what was happening in the present! She had noticed that Doctor Clarice had her toolkit with her, and she asked if the spyglasses were broken.

"No," said Doctor Clarice. "I've been adding a tiny camera to the telescope that looks over Looking-Glass Lake. I just need to tighten these screws, then it's ready to go."

Rosie asked if she could help and Doctor

Clarice looked pleased. "Of course," she said, handing her a screwdriver.

Rosie tightened the screws and beamed when Doctor Clarice told her she was a natural. She looked through the telescope. "It's amazing," she said. "The picture is so clear! I feel as if I could reach out and touch the water."

They took turns watching the lake, but all they could see was the fishergnome in his boat, bobbing about on the waves.

"Never mind," said Doctor Clarice. "I'll set the camera to record, then come back later and check the film." She shivered. "Who knows—maybe whatever we are looking for only comes out at night!"

Kat put her eye to the telescope for one last look. "Wait!" she squeaked. "I can see something splashing around near the shore."

"Quick!" said Doctor Clarice. "Tap the top of the telescope and it will take a photo."

Kat did as she was told, and there was a loud click, followed by a complicated whirring sound.

Doctor Clarice was looking very pleased with herself. "I knew that camera would come in handy," she said. She unscrewed the heart-shaped lens and took out a picture

printed on a small, circular card. "Oh," she said, looking a little disappointed. "That's just a sea dragon."

Kat took the picture and stared at it. "What's a *sea* dragon doing in a lake?" she asked.

"Sea dragons are happy in any kind of water," said Doctor Clarice. "They're gentle creatures, and they're really very friendly. This one's a girl—you can tell by the frill on her neck."

Rosie looked through the spyglass. "Look at how long her tail is!" she said. "It's beautiful, all green and blue like the sea. Let's call her Suki! I'd love to meet her."

"Perhaps you can," said Doctor Clarice. "I think Doctor Hart is planning a trip to the lake tomorrow. I'm sure she'd be happy to have you join her."

They found Doctor Hart in the Potion Room—"Or, my Witch's Kitchen, as I sometimes call it," laughed Doctor Hart. The room *would* have looked very much like a kitchen—if kitchens had shelves full of bottled spiderwebs and crocodile tears! There was a wooden table in the middle of the room covered in teetering stacks of spell books and shiny cauldrons. Kat could also see a barrel of shimmering pixie dust with a toad sitting on the lid! She thought it was one of the most exciting rooms in the surgery.

The toad croaked loudly as they entered the room.

"Don't mind Herbie," said Doctor Hart. "He thinks he's a guard toad!" She scooped a spoonful of leaves into a glass flask and added a drop of pale pink liquid from a bubbling test tube. "Did you have any luck

with the telescopes?"

Doctor Clarice shook her head. "Not yet," she said. "There's not much happening on the surface of the lake. I wish we could see what's going on under the water."

"Aha!" said Doctor Hart. "I thought you might say that ... Which is why I'm mixing up a batch of Bubblehead Brew. It's a special potion that lets people breathe underwater," she explained. "I think it's time to investigate what's going on *under* Looking-Glass Lake."

Chapter 4
A Big Bang

Doctor Hart sent Rosie to the storeroom to find wetsuits and flippers for the trip to the lake. This meant that Kat was left with Doctor Hart and the pink magical potion.

The kindly vet tipped the contents of her glass flask into the cauldron, then picked up a saltshaker with a label that read: "Rainbow's Endings." She shook it over the potion, and glittering flakes drifted into the mixture. A lovely smell filled the room, and her round face crinkled into a smile that showed one bright gold tooth. "Perfect," she said. "Would you mind giving it a stir, Kat?"

Kat hesitated. "Are you sure?" she asked. She wanted to help but, well, things hadn't exactly gone according to plan the last time she stirred one of Doctor Hart's potions.

"Of course I'm sure," replied Doctor Hart. "Just give it a good stir. I'll be watching you."

Watching me? Kat thought nervously. She took a spoon and peered into the cauldron, then glanced back at Doctor Hart, who gave her a big thumbs up. "Here goes," she said, and started to stir.

At once, the potion began to fizz and crackle. Kat gulped as a thin ribbon of pink steam rose toward the ceiling.

"Keep stirring," said Doctor Hart cheerfully. "You're doing a great job! Now try saying the magic words as you stir. It goes like this: *Bubble bright, Water light, Breathing calm, Safe from harm.*"

"I'm not sure I can remember all that," muttered Kat.

"That's not a problem, my dear," said Doctor Hart. "Just repeat the words after me. *Bubble bright ...*"

"Okay," said Kat. "*Bubble bright ...* Eek!" As soon as she spoke the words, the potion began to bubble fiercely, and the thin stream of pink steam got thicker. The air turned pink as the room quickly filled with a choking cloud of sparkling smoke.

"Oh no!" said Kat, putting down the spoon. She took a step away from the cauldron ...

Just in time. There was a loud *BANG!* and even more smoke rushed out of the cauldron. It was so thick now that Kat could hardly see. Coughing and spluttering, she tried to leave the room, but she couldn't figure out where the door was!

"Stay where you are," called Doctor Hart, hurrying across the room to open a window. At once, the smoke started to clear. "Are you alright?" she asked, flapping at the air with the large sunhat she always wore. "I don't know why witches in stories always have those silly pointed black hats. This type is far more useful for clearing away smoke when a spell goes wrong."

Kat gave her a weak smile. "I'm sorry," she said. "I don't know what happened."

There was a croak from the corner of the room, and Kat saw that Herbie the toad had hopped under a bucket to hide.

"Herbie says don't worry," laughed the vet, taking the toad out from under the upturned bucket and plopping him in her pocket. "Things like that happened all the time when I first started learning magic. It won't take long to brew up another batch."

People *keep* telling me not to worry, Kat thought to herself. But it was hard not to worry when things kept going wrong! First the Sing-Song Spell, then the spelling bee—and now this.

Suddenly, there was a strange noise from outside the room. It sounded like an angry lion's roar!

The door flew open to reveal ... Rosie! Her eyes were crossed, her tongue was sticking out, and she was wearing a pair of rubber flippers on her hands. "Grrrr!" she roared.

She looked so silly that Kat couldn't help laughing. "You must be the least scary sea monster in the world," she said.

Rosie had found a whole box of wetsuits and flippers to try on. Kat took a pair of flippers and put them on her own hands. "Now we're matching monsters!" she said. She was glad that she had a good friend like

Rosie to help chase her worries away.

"We'll set off for the lake first thing tomorrow morning," said Doctor Hart.

"Do you think we'll meet a sea dragon?" Kat asked. Ever since she'd seen Suki through the telescope, she had been hoping to meet her up close.

"We might," said Doctor Hart. "They often play near the surface. Sometimes the gnomes get angry, because their games scare the fish away, but they're only having fun."

"I can't *wait* for tomorrow," sighed Rosie. "Lacey would be so jealous if she knew what we were doing."

Kat gave her friend a little hug. She'd already forgotten about the conversation in the schoolyard—but the mean comments had clearly upset Rosie more than she'd realized.

Chapter 5
Suki Gets Stuck

The girls arrived at the surgery bright and early the next morning. Doctor Hart was busy pouring the Bubblehead Brew into bottles, so the girls climbed the spiral staircase to look through the magical spyglasses.

Rosie found the telescope that looked out on the lake. "I can see a sea dragon," she called excitedly. "I think it's Suki!" She passed the spyglass to Kat. The sea dragon was playing in the waves, splashing with her tail, then twirling around as she tried to catch the shimmering drops of water.

"She's having so much fun," laughed

Kat. She was about to hand the spyglass back to Rosie when she noticed a dark shadow behind Suki. Was it just a trick of the light, or was something there? Suddenly, two boggling eyes emerged from the water— but Suki was too busy with her splashing game to notice.

"Look out, Suki!" yelled Kat, even though she knew that the sea dragon was too far away to hear her.

A waving tentacle snaked out of the water and tapped Suki on the tail. But before Kat could think to take a picture, the creature had disappeared beneath the waves again.

"I just saw a monster," Kat gasped.

"Let me see!" said Rosie.

"Okay," said Kat, handing her the telescope. "But tell me what's happening." She hopped anxiously from one foot to the other as Rosie looked at the lake.

"Suki's swimming to the shore ..." said Rosie. "She's climbing out of the lake. I think she's looking for somewhere to hide." She gave the telescope back to Kat. "I couldn't see any monsters."

Kat pressed her eye to the telescope. Rosie was right. The monster was nowhere to be seen—but Suki was scurrying away from the water heading for a row of beach huts. She pushed at each of their doors in turn until one swung open. Then she started to squeeze inside.

The hut was not very big—in fact it was gnome-sized—but Suki was determined to

fit herself in. Buckets, nets, umbrellas, chairs, and fishing rods flew out of the door as she scrabbled to make room.

"I'm not sure that's such a good idea," murmured Kat. She passed the telescope back to Rosie.

"I see what you mean," said Rosie. "Her head's poking out of the door, and her tail's sticking through the window. She's wiggling around to get her tail free, but she can't. Oh no! I think she's stuck!"

The girls raced down the spiral staircase, calling for Doctor Hart. They found her in Doctor Clarice's lab, loading bottles of Bubblehead Brew onto the flying carpet.

"It sounds like I need to bring a Shrink-Me Charm," said Doctor Hart when she had heard Kat's story, and bustled off to fetch one.

"The carpet's still extra bubbly, so we can get there in no time," said Doctor Clarice. Then she grinned. "As long as Doctor Hart doesn't drive, that is!"

Doctor Hart appeared at the door. "Ahem!" she said. "I heard that." Her face crinkled up into an amused smile, and Kat could tell that she was only pretending to be angry.

"Are you really a bad driver?" asked Rosie.

"Let's just say I'm not as good as Doctor Clarice," said Doctor Hart, "and she's always teasing me about it."

Kat was surprised. "I thought you were good at everything," she said.

"No one in the world is good at *everything*," laughed Doctor Hart. "We all have different strengths and weaknesses. I am very good at spells and potions—but put me in charge of a carpet, and you'll be in for a bumpy ride!"

The flying carpet zoomed high above the trees in a stream of rainbow bubbles, and landed beside the beach huts. Kat had never been this close to Looking-Glass Lake before, although she had flown over it many times. It was a beautiful sight! The water was like a mirror, perfectly reflecting the blue sky and thick, green forest that surrounded it. Tiny waves lapped at the sandy shore, which was studded with glittering shells and stones.

Suki saw them arrive and gave a small roar. Her tail was tightly wedged in the window and wouldn't budge!

"Oh, you poor thing," said Doctor Hart. "We'll have you out in no time." She rummaged in her bag and took out a pot of yellow ointment. "This will only make her tail smaller for a few seconds," she told the girls. "So when you see it shrinking, give it

a push!" She gave Suki a pat, then started
rubbing the slippery ointment onto her tail.

"Now!" called Doctor Clarice.

Magical yellow stars flickered in the air,
and the girls pushed Suki's tail back through
the window. Moments later, the sea dragon
tumbled out of the hut with a full-sized tail
again. She was very dusty—and had several
fishing nets tangled around her—but other
than that, she was unharmed.

The sea dragon stood very still and let Rosie and Kat untangle the fishing nets from her neck and tail. She gave a happy snort when the nets were gone and licked Kat's face—making her giggle!

Doctor Clarice wiped the dust off Suki's back with a wet cloth and gave her a little pat on the back. "You're ready to go back in the lake now," she said cheerfully.

But Suki didn't want to go back into the lake. As soon as the girls tried to encourage her into the water, she started to shiver. She stayed well away from the lake's edge and wouldn't put even a single paw in.

"Don't worry, Suki," said Kat stroking her. "You don't have to go back ... Does she, Doctor Hart?"

"No ..." said Doctor Hart. "But she can't stay out here in the sun. She needs somewhere

cool and damp where she can rest."

Rosie had already spotted some rocky caves further along the shore. "How about in there?" she suggested.

Suki liked it in the dark cave. She curled up on a bed of soft, green seaweed and gave a contented sigh.

"I'll stay and look after her until she feels better," said Doctor Clarice.

Doctor Hart and the girls changed into their wetsuits and sat at the edge of the lake, dipping their toes in the warm water. Doctor Hart took out three bottles of Bubblehead Brew and passed them around.

"I'll go first," said Doctor Hart, taking a sip of the potion. At once, a large, wobbly bubble appeared all around her head—including her flowery sunhat! She waded into the water and smiled up at the girls. "Now it's your turn," she said.

Kat was surprised to find that the potion tasted like strawberries. The world in front of her shimmered for a moment, then cleared. She put a hand up to her face to make sure that the bubble was really there, and it quivered under her fingers. It was like touching a bubble in a sink—except it didn't pop!

"Here I come," she giggled, and jumped into the lake with a huge splash. Rosie followed right behind.

Kat ducked down under the water and found that she could see and hear just as clearly as if she was on land. "Where do we start looking?" she asked excitedly.

"Good question," beamed Doctor Hart. "I think we should pay a visit ... to the mer-elves!"

Chapter 6
Under Looking-Glass Lake

Kat loved swimming—and being able breathe underwater was a dream come true. Rosie took longer to get used to the strange new feeling, but after a while, they were both ready to dive under the lake with Doctor Hart.

The water was so clear that the girls could see all the way down to the soft sand at the bottom. Bright fish darted here and there among the swaying seaweed.

Kat couldn't wait to meet a mer-elf. She had met elves before—and even had an elf friend called Lunella, who sent her postcards from a castle in the clouds—but she hadn't known *mer-elves* even existed! "Can they breathe water?" she asked. "Do they have tails? Are there *other* kinds of mer-creatures?"

"Yes, yes, and yes," laughed Doctor Hart. "Look, there's a mer-bear just over there."

Kat was delighted to see a little bear with a fishy tail playing in the seaweed, and they all stopped to say hello.

They continued swimming, and Kat was surprised to be overtaken by a fish with a big red nose and funny hat. "It looks just like a clown," she said.

"You're quite right," said Doctor Hart. "It's a magical clownfish. In fact, it's probably part of an underwater circus. Look—there's the ringmaster."

A fish in a black top hat swam past, closely followed by a fish juggling seashells. The clownfish pretended to bump into a rock, then started swimming upside-down. It was very funny! It blew a big, shiny bubble that popped with a silly noise. *Honk! Honk!*

As they swam deeper, the sand at the bottom of the lake became rockier. Up ahead, Kat saw an archway made of sparkling shells set into a thick wall of green seaweed. Streams of fish swam in and out, like cars on a busy road.

"That's the entrance to Kelp Town," said Doctor Hart.

Through the archway, the streets were lined with smooth stones and polished glass. Each house was made of white marble with a braided seaweed roof, and everywhere Kat looked, she could see elves with long, scaly tails putting up garlands of seaweed and hanging strings of twinkling lights.

"It's beautiful," breathed Rosie.

"Oh yes," came a snooty voice from behind them. "That is, if you like *homemade* decorations!"

Kat turned to see two mer-elves swimming through the archway. From the look on their faces—and the expensive-looking jewels that they were wearing—Kat realized that they did *not* like homemade decorations at all.

"Hello," said Doctor Hart in a friendly voice. "Do you live here?"

The two elves collapsed into peals of laughter, as if they'd heard a very funny joke.

"Us? Live here?" gasped the lady. "I am Lady Fitz-Seaweed, and this is my husband, Lord Barnacle. This ... *pond* ... isn't even big enough for our seahorse stables."

This made Doctor Hart raise her eyebrows in surprise. "Er ... I see," she said.

"We're tourists," explained Lord Barnacle, shaking the vet's hand. "We've come for the Pearl Moon Festival."

"Goodness, is that what all these decorations are for?" said Doctor Hart. She turned to the girls. "When the Pearl Moon shines over Starfall Forest, the giant oysters on the lake bed open up to reveal their shining, magical pearls. It creates an incredible light show—but it only happens on one night every hundred years!"

"There's a big parade too," said Lord Barnacle. "And lots of tasty treats—"

He was interrupted by a shout from another mer-elf, who was swimming toward them holding a tangle of fairy lights. Her tail was a brilliant blue, and her long blonde hair cascaded around her shoulders. Kat thought she looked like a mermaid from a fairy story.

"Sorry to keep you waiting," she called. "It has been so busy with the Pearl Moon Festival preparations!"

"And who," said Lady Fitz-Seaweed, "are you?"

"I'm the head of the Kelp Town Tourist Welcome Committee," said the mer-elf. "My name's Sirena. It's my job to welcome visitors to the Pearl Moon Festival." She hurried over to the shell archway and draped the lights around it. "I meant to put these up yesterday, but I've been so busy," she said. "You see, I'm also the head of the Kelp Town Decoration Committee. We spent all day sorting out the garlands."

"Have you brought some nice ones too?" asked Lady Fitz-Seaweed.

"Oh no," said Sirena, looking a little embarrassed. "We made them ourselves. Kelp Town is not a very grand place, I'm afraid ... But we've all worked hard to decorate the town and make costumes for the big parade."

"I love the decorations," said Rosie warmly.

"Oh thank you," said Sirena. "Are you all tourists too?"

"No, no," said Doctor Hart. "We're from Calico Comfrey's Veterinary Surgery. Something new has come to live in this lake, and it's scaring the other creatures. Have you heard anything about it?"

Sirena looked shocked. "No!" she said. "Nothing. Not one thing."

Suddenly, Kat's nose started to itch. She looked at Rosie and saw that her friend had the same problem!

"Oh dear," said Doctor Hart. "An itchy nose means that the potion is wearing off. We need to get back to the surface right away."

"You can come back tomorrow if you like," said Sirena. "I'll ask around and let you know if I find out anything."

They said goodbye and swam back to the surface. As soon as their heads popped out of the water, their head bubbles disappeared.

"It looks like I'll need to whip up another batch of Bubblehead Brew," Doctor Hart said thoughtfully. "Can you come back and help me, Kat?"

Kat thought about the thick, pink smoke that had filled the room the day before. "Sorry," she said. "I'm a bit tired."

Kat was very quiet on the way home. She wanted to talk to Rosie about something important, but she couldn't do it while the vets were listening.

As soon as the enchanted gate swung shut behind them, she turned to her friend. "Why does Doctor Hart keep asking *me* to help with her potions?" she asked.

Rosie looked astonished. "Don't you *want* to help?" she asked.

"Of course I do," said Kat quickly. "But I keep messing things up."

"I don't understand," said Rosie.

"You wouldn't," Kat said. "You find *everything* so easy."

"No I don't," Rosie said indignantly.

"Yes, you do!" Kat suddenly felt very angry. "*You* didn't make the potion bubble over," she said. "And *you* didn't fill the surgery

with smoke. And you won the spelling bee
without even trying."

Rosie frowned. "I thought you were
happy for me," she said.

"I was," said Kat. "It's just that ... I spent
forever trying to learn the words, and I was
still the first person to sit down."

"You worried about it too much," said
Rosie. "Spelling bees are meant to be fun."

"You see?" shouted Kat. "You just don't
get it!"

Rosie gasped and Kat suddenly felt terrible. "I'm sorry," she said. "I didn't mean to shout."

"That's okay," said Rosie stiffly.

The girls walked through the yard in silence. Kat's mind was in a whirl. She wanted to tell Rosie about Miss Lavender— and the meeting with her parents—and how scared she was that she might be sent to another school ... But now she couldn't. If only she hadn't lost her temper.

When they reached the back door, Rosie's dad was waiting for them. He held up his hands and wiggled his fingers.

"What is he doing?" Kat asked.

"Playing an invisible piano," said Rosie. "He's telling me it's time for piano practice."

Kat smiled as Rosie's dad started puffing out his cheeks and pretending to play a trumpet. "Do you have trumpet practice too?" she asked.

"No," sighed Rosie. "Now he's showing off."

"Your dad's loopy," giggled Kat.

"I know," said Rosie, and they both laughed.

"I'm sorry things keep going wrong for you," Rosie said. "Friends?"

Kat felt very relieved. "Friends," she said. "I'll see you tomorrow."

When Kat got back home, she went straight up to her bedroom. Two of her hamsters were running noisily in their wheel, while the other two were curled up in a corner fast asleep. She opened the door and Eenie scurried onto her hand, then up her arm to her shoulder. She scooped up Meenie too and let him snuggle into her—leaving Miney and Moe to doze.

Her mother came into the room and smiled

to see her daughter covered in hamsters! "Hi Kat," she said. "I've just been on the phone with your teacher."

Kat carefully put the hamsters back into the cage and closed the door. She felt a lump forming in her throat.

"She's asked us to come in for a meeting on Monday," her mother continued. "She says you've been struggling a bit in class."

Kat nodded miserably. "I keep messing things up," she said. Then it all came tumbling out. The spelling bee, the ruined potions—and the fight with Rosie.

Mama listened patiently and, when Kat finished, she scooped her up into an enormous hug. "I'm sorry you've been having such a tough time," she said. "But listen. Do you know what I see when I look at you?"

"What do you see?" sniffed Kat.

"I see Kat the Magnificent," said Mama with a big smile. "Kat the Mighty. Kat the Magical!"

This made Kat laugh. "Really?"

"Really," said Mama. "And you know what else? I'm sure that's what Doctor Hart sees too."

"So should I keep helping with her potions?" Kat asked.

"Well, people do say mistakes help you learn ..." replied her mother.

Kat thought for a moment and decided that the next time Doctor Hart asked her to help, she would say yes. Suddenly, her tummy gave a loud rumble.

"All that swimming has made you hungry," laughed Mama. "I'm cooking baked macaroni and cheese for dinner.

Would you like to help?"

"Yes please!" Kat followed her mother downstairs to the kitchen and switched on the radio. A burst of pop music blared out from the speakers.

Mama picked up a wooden spoon and pretended it was a microphone. "Ooh, I love this song!" she said.

"Me too," said Kat, grabbing a spoon and singing along.

Chapter 7
Chaos in Kelp Town

The sun shone brightly the next day. Looking-Glass Lake was so clear and still that it was hard to imagine anything scary lurking deep below the water!

Kat's crystalzoometer started buzzing as soon as she arrived at the lake. It didn't take long to see the problem! A group of baby trootles were crawling into the forest.

"If they wander too far, they'll get lost," said Doctor Hart. "Baby trootles need to stay close to the water."

Rosie and Kat started to round up the trootles, gently steering each one back in

the direction of the lake. Every trootle had a miniature island on its back, just like the one they had seen at the surgery. At last, all the tiny trootles had waddled into the water.

"Phew!" panted Kat. "That's the last one." She paused looking puzzled. "So why is my crystalzoometer still spinning?"

Rosie took hers out of her pocket. "Mine is too," she said. "It's pointing in the direction of that cave," she said. "Isn't that where we left Suki?"

The girls climbed carefully over the slippery rocks that lined the cave entrance.

"Suki?" Kat called. Her voice echoed when she said the sea dragon's name.

There was a watery roar from the darkness, and Suki came scampering out to greet them. She was delighted to see the two girls again and bounded in circles around them, butting them gently with her curved horns.

"She seems fine," said Kat in a puzzled voice. "Perhaps the crystalzoometer made a mistake." Then she reached out a hand to stroke Suki's scaly tail. "That's not right," she exclaimed. The scales felt dry and dusty.

"She must have been out of the water for too long," Rosie said. "Are you still too scared to go back in the lake, Suki?"

The sea dragon nodded her head.

Kat thought for a moment, then picked up

a long strand of wavy seaweed. "This should help," she said.

Rosie understood what her friend was doing and started to hunt for more slimy strips. Soon, Suki was covered in seaweed.

"That will help keep your skin moist for now," Kat said with a sigh. "But you'll have to go back into the water *some* time ..."

The girls left the cave and found Doctor Hart sitting under a tree with her nose buried in an ancient-looking spell book.

"I've just had a wonderful idea," she said. "We can use a Finding Spell to show us exactly where this creature is. I've not tried one before, but it's all in this book! We don't even need to go back to the surgery for any ingredients. Everything we need is right here."

Rosie peered over her shoulder at the list of ingredients. "A cauldron of water, twenty purple pebbles, and a shell filled with sand," she read. "No problem!"

Rosie found a bucket and started to collect smooth, purple pebbles from the water's edge, while Kat hunted around for the perfect shell. In no time at all, they had everything they needed. Doctor Hart laid the pebbles in a star shape around the cauldron. Then, she poured the sand into the water and stirred it with the shell.

"What happens now?" Kat asked excitedly.

"Oh dear," said Doctor Hart, looking at the spell book. "We have to leave it in the sunlight for at least an hour to brew. Never mind!" She shut the book cheerfully. "We can see if Sirena discovered anything about the creature while we wait."

The girls changed into their wetsuits, slipped on their flippers, and drank some Bubblehead Brew. It tasted like watermelon.

"I changed the recipe a bit," Doctor Hart admitted. "It should last longer this time."

As they swam toward Kelp Town, it was clear that something was wrong. The streets were packed with panicking mer-elves, bumping into each other in their haste. Fish were darting into the seaweed and crabs were scuttling under rocks to hide.

Suddenly, they saw Lady Fitz-Seaweed swimming toward them. "Help!" she squeaked. "There's a m-m-m-monster on the loose!" She dived into a clump of seaweed, then poked her head out again. "You'd better get in here too!" she hissed.

Doctor Hart ushered Kat and Rosie into the waving fronds, then climbed in herself.

"Did it attack you?" asked Doctor Hart.

"N-no," said the mer-elf. "But it's terrifying—as big as a whale, with huge eyes and long tentacles. It said *GRRRRRRRRRRRAGGGH*! Then it disappeared in a cloud of black ink."

"Hmm," said Doctor Hart. "That sounds like the creature that scared Suki. I've seen the picture from Doctor Clarice's clever telescope camera. The trouble is, I can't work out *what* it is."

Kat peeped out of the seaweed to see if she could spot the monster. But all she saw was Sirena holding a megaphone to her mouth.

"Attention everyone!" Sirena boomed. "As head of the Keep Kelp Town Safe Committee, I am pleased to tell you that the monster has gone."

All the mer-elves started to swim out from their hiding places, and Kat swam out to join them.

"It looks like you were right about there being a monster," Sirena sadly told her.

Doctor Hart spotted a baby chattersnake that had tied itself in knots trying to hide and paddled over to help. Its pink and yellow scales were very slippery, and it took her a while to get it free. Just before it wriggled away, the chattersnake blew out a stream of pretty pink bubbles in the shape of a heart.

"Chattersnakes talk by blowing bubble pictures," said Doctor Hart. "That meant *thank you*." She pursed her lips and blew some bubbles of her own in the shape of a smiling face. "And this means you're welcome."

"You speak Chattersnake? How wonderful!" Sirena said. "Now, if you will excuse me, I have an important announcement to make."

Sirena solemnly gathered the mer-elves into a group. "It is my sad duty to inform you that the Pearl Moon Festival will not be going ahead," she said. "All tourists must leave Kelp Town right away."

There was an angry muttering from the assembled mer-elves.

"But there won't be another Pearl Moon for one hundred years," said one.

"It took me four days to swim here," grumbled another.

"I'm sorry," replied Sirena, shaking her head. "It's just too dangerous. Didn't you see the monster? It looked like this ..." She screwed up her face into a scary expression. "And it said *GRRRRRRRRAGGGH*!"

All the mer-elves stopped muttering and looked very frightened.

Doctor Hart swam over and put her arm around Sirena's shoulders. "Now, now," she said. "Don't be so hasty. We don't know what this creature wants yet. Perhaps it is lost or hurt and needs our help."

"Perhaps," said Sirena doubtfully.

"I've got a Finding Spell brewing up on land," said Doctor Hart. "It should be ready now. I can use it to track down this creature and find out what is going on."

As they swam back to the surface, Kat kept watch for any sign of tentacles or googly eyes, but there was no sign of the monster anywhere.

Near the surface, they swam through a cloud of fish that looked like floating sandwiches with tiny black eyes. Their little brown fins tickled Kat as they brushed past her. She tried to avoid them, but there were

too many whirling and twirling around. None of them seemed to know which way they were going, or what they were doing.

"Dear me," tutted Doctor Hart. "These peanut-butter-and-jellyfish seem a little confused! They usually spend all their time in the caves at the bottom of the lake."

"I bet the monster scared *them* too," said Rosie.

They had nearly reached the shore when Kat's nose started to itch. "The potion's wearing off," she said. She waded out of the lake and took off her flippers, wriggling her toes in the warm sand. Rosie flopped down beside her and did the same. A spotty pink crab scuttled past them snapping its pincers in the air. It stopped for a moment, and stared at the girls, then raced away into a rock pool.

Chapter 8
A Special Spell

The water in the cauldron had turned a deep orange. "That means it's ready to use," said Doctor Hart. "If the spell works, then anyone the creature has touched will be able to lead us straight to it. I'm rather hoping Suki will lend us a paw ..."

"We'll go and fetch her," said Kat.

The sea dragon was pleased to see her new friends. She jumped up as soon as they entered the cave and scampered around, swishing her tail. Sea dragons were as smart as they were playful, and Suki listened attentively as Kat explained what they needed her to do as

they walked to the sandy shore.

"Will you help?" Rosie softly asked. Suki nodded her scaly head.

Doctor Hart looked up from her spell book as they approached. "I've just been reading the small print," she said. "This Finding Spell can only be performed by two witches working together." She snapped the book shut and looked straight at Kat. "I'm going to need your help, my dear."

Kat's heart started to beat fast. "I'm not a witch," she said.

"Not yet," admitted Doctor Hart. "A witch is someone who has been trained to use magic. But before she can be trained, she has to have that magic inside her." The vet took out a wooden spoon and handed it to Kat. "You stir the potion and I'll read out the magic words."

"No," said Kat. "Wait. I can't be magic. Every time I've tried to help you, it's gone wrong. When I stirred the spell for the singing starfish, it bubbled all over the table ..."

Doctor Hart smiled. "That was what gave me the idea," she said. "Only someone with magic inside them could have made it explode like that! That's why I asked you to help with the Bubblehead Brew ..."

"You wanted to see if it would happen

again and it did," said Kat. "All that smoke!"

"I didn't want to raise your hopes until I was completely sure," said Doctor Hart. "But now I am. What do you think? Can you help me one more time?"

Kat gulped nervously. Then she remembered her mother's words. Of course I can, she thought. I'm Kat the Magnificent. Kat the Mighty ... Kat the *Magical!*

She picked up the cauldron and started to stir.

Rosie and Suki sat on a rock and waited to see what would happen.

Doctor Hart read out the magic words: "*Shell and sand, Lend a hand, Stones and air, Take us there!*"

BOOM! A loud noise exploded out of the cauldron and the potion began to bubble. There was a sudden flash of bright, white light and Kat squeezed her eyes tightly shut.

When she opened them again, the potion had turned back into water and sand. She stopped stirring and let the sand settle at the bottom of the cauldron. It hasn't worked, she thought sadly. *Doctor Hart was wrong. I've messed up again ...*

But Doctor Hart didn't look at all upset. She started to dance around the rocks, kicking up the sand with her feet and shouting happily. "You did it!" she sang. "It works!"

"It works?" Kat slowly asked.

"Look at Suki!" replied Doctor Hart.

Kat looked around and saw that the sea dragon was glowing with a strange, orange light. Suki stared at her paws, one by one, with a puzzled look on her face.

Doctor Hart stopped dancing and gave Kat an enormous hug. "You've got magic inside you, Kat. You're going to be an *incredible* witch some day."

"I still don't believe it," said Kat.

"I do!" said Rosie. She threw her arms around her friend and gave her a squeeze. "I'm so excited for you!"

Kat returned the hug with a huge smile. "You're such a great friend," she said. "I'm sorry I haven't been much fun to hang out with lately. The thing is ..." And then, finally, she told Rosie all about the meeting with Miss Lavender.

"I didn't know you found it so *hard* to learn the words for the spelling bee," said Rosie. "I could have helped you study."

"Maybe next time," said Kat. Then she shuddered. "Although, I hope there's not another spelling bee for a *very* long time!"

Beside them, Suki gave a little snort and pawed at the ground.

"She wants to get going," said Doctor Hart.

"We're ready too," said Rosie, stroking the sea dragon's glimmering neck.

Doctor Hart looked solemn. "Are you absolutely sure you want to come?" she asked. "I believe that this mysterious creature is just misunderstood, but ... well. It does seem rather good at scaring people."

Kat and Rosie looked at each other, and grinned. "If Suki is brave enough to go then so are we," they said.

Chapter 9
The Monster's Cave

Poor Suki! It was clear that she really wanted to help Doctor Hart and the girls—but, at the same time, she was nervous about getting into the water. She paced up and down at the lake's edge.

"Maybe we should go first," Rosie said.

Doctor Hart agreed. She took a sip of Bubblehead Brew and hopped into the lake. "Come on, Suki," she said in an encouraging voice. "Sea dragons belong in the water."

"Look at me, Suki!" said Rosie, jumping into the lake with a loud splash.

"Wait for me," said Kat, diving in after her.

At last, Suki seemed to make her mind up. She swished her tail, closed her eyes, took a step forward, and … jumped!

"Good job, Suki!" cheered Kat.

Once Suki was in the water, there was no looking back—she was in her element! She swam in circles around Rosie and Kat, splashing them with her tail. She flipped and turned like an underwater gymnast, then paddled back and nudged the girls with her snout—just to make sure that they'd been watching!

Doctor Hart and the girls followed Suki across Looking-Glass Lake. She swam high above Kelp Town, which was close to the shore, and headed for the middle of the lake where the water was deepest.

The lake bed twinkled under Kat's kicking flippers, and she saw that they were swimming above a series of underwater caves. Each one was lined with sparkling blue gemstones.

"Aha," said Doctor Hart. "So our creature is hiding out in the Cloudless Caves."

Suki dived under the water with Doctor Hart and the girls right behind. The sunlight bouncing off the crystals made the water so bright that Kat had to squint to see the caves properly. Some were too small to fit anything larger than a baby trootle, but some were enormous—the perfect place for something big and scary to hide.

Suki swam from cave to cave, pausing
every now and then to sniff the seaweed,
then came to a stop outside the entrance to
the biggest cave.

"Have you noticed the fish?" Kat asked.

Rosie looked around her and frowned.
"I can't see *any* fish," she said.

"Exactly!" said Kat. "I bet there were
hundreds of fish living here—until the
monster moved in ..."

Suddenly, a loud roar filled the water, and Suki shot away from the cave entrance.

"Was that the monster?" said Rosie, putting her arm around Suki's neck to comfort her. "It doesn't sound happy!"

"No, it doesn't, poor thing," agreed Doctor Hart. "Luckily, I know a Whistling Charm that will calm any living creature. I learned it from my grandfather, Calico Comfrey ... and he learned it from the Whistling Warlocks."

The vet pursed her lips and started to whistle a strange tune. It sounded like the same four notes repeated over and over again, slow at first, then a little faster. Kat thought it was the most relaxing thing she had ever heard. All her worries started to melt away, leaving her with a warm, calm feeling.

"Well, it's working on us," said Rosie

dreamily. Even Suki looked calmer, swimming
over to nestle against Doctor Hart's legs.

Then—*GRRRRRRRRRAGGGH*! Another
roar burst out of the cave.

"Oh no!" said Rosie. "It's still angry."

"But that's impossible," said Doctor Hart.
"That charm always works! There must be
something *very* unusual about this creature."

GRRRRRRRRRRAGH! The roar rang out again, and Suki gave a little whimper.

"Don't be scared," said Kat. "Doctor Hart will know what to do."

Doctor Hart swam close to the cave's entrance and peered inside. "Hello!" she called. "We're here to help. Please come out. We won't hurt you!" She pursed her lips and whistled the magical charm again.

All at once, Kat understood that the kindly vet really *was* concerned about this creature. She had never once called it a "monster"— even though everyone else had! Doctor Hart loved all creatures equally—magical and nonmagical, big and small.

The water around them rippled as something moved in the darkness at the back of the cave. Then, very slowly, an enormous creature started making its way toward them. It had a strange, round body and huge eyes that stood out on stalks on the top of its head. Long, wavy tentacles brushed the crystal-covered walls of the cave as it shuffled forward.

Suki took one look at the creature and fled.

"Come back, Suki!" called Rosie. But the sea dragon raced away through the water, cowering behind the wreck of a fishing boat that was upturned on the lake floor.

The monster crept out of its cave with another loud roar. Kat gulped and clutched Rosie's arm, as the creature's long tentacles swished angrily around, churning up the water. But Doctor Hart was staring at the creature in amazement.

"I've never seen anything like it in my life," she said. "Could it be that we have discovered an entirely new species of animal?"

"Doctor Hart—look out!" Rosie called. There was a hissing noise and the monster sent out a jet of ink into the water, turning it black.

"Well I never," said Doctor Hart. "Roar like a dragon, eyes like a crab, as big as a whale ... and now it's shooting ink like a squid! How very extraordinary." She tried to get a better look, but the monster turned around and shot backward out of the cave. Its dangling tentacles whipped through the water, thumping against the wall as they went.

Kat flattened herself against the crystals to let it pass. She managed to avoid the swinging tentacles but scraped her leg on a piece of blue crystal that was jutting out.

"Ouch!" she said.

Suki gave a little growl and crept out from behind the upturned fishing boat. She clearly didn't like the idea of her friends being hurt.

"Don't worry, Suki," Kat said. "It's only a graze. I'm fine."

But Suki swam past her, diving through the monster's tentacles until she was face-to-face with the enormous creature. Then she lowered her head and gave it a huge bump with her curved, white horns.

What happened next was a surprise to everyone!

The monster opened its mouth. But—it wasn't a mouth. Kat could see no sharp teeth, no pink tongue ... In fact, nothing at all. She swam up to the black hole and peered inside.

"It's a door!" she called. "Come and see. I don't think this is a monster at all."

Kat swam through the door, followed by Rosie and Doctor Hart. She found herself in a small, round room made of shiny metal. Everywhere she looked there were levers, buttons, monitors, dials, and switches. Tiny lights in the ceiling flickered red and orange, and there was a bucket of black ink and a hose on the floor.

Someone was sitting at the steering wheel.

"Oh my stars!" said Doctor Hart. "Sirena?"

The mer-elf turned to face them. "Hello," she said in a small voice.

Doctor Hart put her hands on her hips. "Let me guess," she said. "You're head of Kelp Town's Scare Everyone Silly Committee!"

Sirena's pink cheeks flushed with embarrassment, and she shook her head.

"I think you need to tell us what's been going on," said the vet in a gentle tone.

"I didn't want to hurt anyone," Sirena

mumbled. "I just wanted to scare people a little bit. Then I'd have a reason to cancel the Pearl Moon Festival."

Kat was confused. "But why would you want to do that?" she asked. "You worked so hard to make all those decorations."

"They weren't good enough," wailed Sirena. "People kept talking about how *special* our celebration had to be. Everything had to be perfect, but nothing was."

Kat started to feel sorry for Sirena. She remembered how rude Lady Fitz-Seaweed had been about the decorations.

"I built this machine to lead a parade," said Sirena. "But then I changed my mind ... I just wanted to make everyone go away."

"I'm sorry that you felt so upset," said Doctor Hart. "But did you stop to think about all the water creatures you were scaring?"

Sirena listened with a glum expression as Doctor Hart told her about all the animals that had been brought into the surgery.

"I'm sorry," said Sirena. "I don't know why I paid any attention to those stuck-up tourists. I love Kelp Town! I'm proud to live here—and I am proud of our beautiful, homemade decorations."

"Well, that's more like it! Even though your creature is quite scary, it's also an incredible invention—just as detailed and special as your decorations!"

Sirena smiled. "Will you come to the Festival tomorrow night? I suppose I'll have to tell everyone what I did. But I can paint a new, friendly face on this monster to show them it's not scary after all."

Sirena swam outside to apologize to Suki with a handful of seaweed candy. Suki gobbled it up, then twirled around.

Kat laughed. "I think Suki's forgiven you."

"I'm so pleased," said Sirena. Then she stared at Doctor Hart. "Is there something wrong with your nose?"

Kat looked at Doctor Hart—who was wriggling her nose up and down—and suddenly realized that her own nose was feeling itchy too. "The Bubblehead Brew is wearing off," she said. "It's time to go home."

Chapter 10
The Pearl Moon Festival

Not long ago, Kat had been very worried about her parents' meeting with Miss Lavender. But a lot had happened since then. Now, the world felt more ... magical. She wasn't exactly *worried* any more—but she wasn't looking forward to it either!

On the way to school, all Rosie could talk about was the Pearl Moon Festival. She was still chattering about it in the classroom. "I can't wait to see Suki again," she whispered to Kat.

"Who?" said Kat, who hadn't been listening.

"*Suki.* Sea dragon. Remember?" Rosie waggled her fingers as if they were horns.

At the front of the classroom, Miss Lavender clapped her hands to get everyone's attention. "Good morning, Rainbow Class," she said. "Let's give a nice welcome to Mr. Binns, the vice principal."

All eyes turned to stare at the man standing beside her. He gave them a cheery wave.

"Mr. Binns has kindly agreed to sit with you for the next lesson," said Miss Lavender. "Kat, can you come with me, please?"

Kat sat with her parents in the school office. Miss Lavender sat on the other side of the table with a handful of glossy leaflets.

"As you know, Kat is a good student, but she has been struggling with some parts of her studies," said the teacher. "I think it's possible that she has dyslexia."

"What is ... dyslexia?" said Kat.

"People with dyslexia can be talented and smart, but they find reading and writing hard," said Miss Lavender. "That would explain why spelling is tricky for you." She smiled at Kat. "There are tests we can do to find out for sure. If I'm right, there are lots of things we can do to help."

Kat gulped. "Will I have to go to a different school?" she asked.

Miss Lavender stared at her in surprise. "A different school?" she said. "Of course not. Whatever gave you that idea?"

"I don't know," said Kat. She felt as if a huge weight had been taken off her shoulders.

"I know it's a lot to think about," Miss Lavender said. "Just remember, we're here to help. You're a fine student, and we're proud to have you here."

"We're proud of her too," said Kat's mother.

On the way out, Kat's parents stopped to look at the display board in the classroom.

Kat showed them the picture of the swimming pool, and Mama said it was very good. "I could just dive into that pool!" she said. Then she gave Kat a little hug. "Everything's going to be alright, you know," she said.

"I know," said Kat. Miss Lavender was right —there was a lot for her to think about. But knowing that her parents and teachers were on her side made everything feel better.

"Where's Rosie's picture?" asked Dad. "Ah, here it is. All about playing the piano. Nice."

"Some of the other kids laughed at her," said Kat. "They said it was a boring hobby."

"Oh, did they now?" said Dad, raising his eyebrows. "And what did those kids write about?"

Kat pointed to Lacey's picture. "Lacey Goldstone got a pony for her birthday," she said.

To her surprise, this made her dad laugh. "No, she didn't," he said.

"What?" Kat frowned. "How do you know?"

"I work with Mr. Goldstone," Dad said. "Lacey's dad. He talks about his daughter all the time. He told me that he got her a science kit for her birthday. It sounds like she made up the pony to show off!"

Kat said goodbye to her parents and dashed out into the yard where the rest of her class was playing Boombadger Tag.

"Was the meeting okay?" Rosie asked. "What happened?"

"I'll tell you later," smiled Kat. "Everything's going to be fine. But you'll never guess what I found out about Lacey!" She was so excited to explain what her dad had said, that she didn't realize Dexter was listening too …

"Is that true?" giggled Dexter. "Hey, Lacey!" he called. "Have you been *pretending* to have a pony?"

Lacey's face flushed red. "How did you know?" she said.

"No way!" said Megan, making a shocked face. "That's so embarrassing. Why would you make up a story like that?"

Lacey stared at the ground as if she wished

it would swallow her up.

"Leave her alone," Rosie said suddenly. "I bet she made it up because you two are always talking about how *exciting* your hobbies are. But it's okay to like science experiments—or playing the piano."

Lacey gave her a grateful smile, and all the other children nodded in agreement.

"I like collecting rocks," said one boy.

Kat smiled and squeezed Rosie's hand. "That was really brave of you," she whispered.

That night, Doctor Clarice picked up the girls from Willow Cottage on the flying carpet. Doctor Hart was waiting by Looking-Glass Lake with the Bubblehead Brew.

Sirena met them at the shell archway and hurried them into the town. "You're just in time," she said. "The parade is beginning."

Kat could hear the sound of music echoing around the rocks. Then the parade came into sight led by Sirena's mechanical monster. A group of mer-elf children were riding on its back, and she had painted a huge smile on its face just like she'd promised.

"I can hardly believe that's our scary monster," laughed Doctor Clarice. "No wonder we couldn't tell what sort of creature it was."

There were elves playing drums and flutes, elves waving flags and balloons, and elves

whirling and twirling their sparkling tails through the water as they danced past. Everyone had dressed up for the show with homemade pendants, bracelets, rings, and tiaras made of delicate shells.

"This is fantastic!" said Rosie.

"I suppose it *is* rather good," said Lady Fitz-Seaweed, as she floated past arm in arm with Lord Barnacle.

"Look, there's Suki," said Kat excitedly.

Suki had been swimming at the back of the parade playing with the baby seahorses. When she spotted Kat and Rosie, she darted over and nudged them with her snout.

"I think she wants us to follow her," laughed Rosie.

The sea dragon led the girls away from the crowds and over to the wavy seaweed wall that surrounded Kelp Town. Then, with a little smile, she dived into it.

"There's a secret tunnel!" gasped Rosie.

The sea dragon led them up through a twisting green passage and onto a platform of pink rock. At once, Kat realized why they were here. "This is the best view of the giant oysters in the whole lake," she said. "And look! They're starting to open."

Sure enough, the large shells creaked slowly open to reveal the treasures hidden inside. The light of the Pearl Moon streamed through the water and bounced off the magical pearls in a million luminous shades. Tiny silver pinpricks of light dotted the water like stars and, for a moment, Kat felt dizzy, as if the world had turned upside-down and she was falling into the night sky.

The girls watched the lights flash and swirl in amazed silence until the very last oyster closed and the water became dark again.

"Back to sleep for one hundred years," said Rosie with a yawn.

"You or the oysters?" Kat giggled. "I'm almost too tired to swim back to the surface."

At once, Suki darted away, returning with one of the garlands from the parade wrapped around her. She let the girls grab hold, then set off at top speed, pulling the girls behind her until they reached the shore.

"We must be the luckiest girls in the world," said Rosie sleepily—and Kat couldn't help but agree.